How to Make Great
Training Videos

6 steps to making great training videos for your organisation or Corporations

Jack Max

How to make great training videos

Table of Content

INTRODUCTION

Video is one of the most mainstream approaches to convey and use content on the web over the years. That is not changing this year 2020.

Instagram, Twitter, Facebook and YouTube all urge individuals to watch and offer short, casual recorded videos. Also, your clients are searching for recordings, usually video content, to take care of their issues like never before.

As a matter of facts and reality, as per a Pew Research study, over 80% of clients said that YouTube is significant for helping them make sense of how to do things they were unable to do previously.

In this way, it's an obvious fact that video is very significant. Also, this makes clients specially open to your services and product through your video content as they attempt to get familiar with your products and services.

This simply implies that mentors, instructional planners, and any other individual entrusted with preparing clients ought to make instructional video content as a major aspect of their client training program.

The most effective method to making great and effective instructional or training videos

In this book, I'll take you through key strides to making effective training videos.

CHAPTER 1

What a Training video is.

A training video, regardless of whether a worker training video or client training, is a video committed to instructing watchers on a particular point with the objective of showing an ability, approach or information.

Basically, it's video-based substance that tells somebody the best way to accomplish something.

Why make training videos for your corporation this year?

How to make great training videos

In case you're asking why you ought to try and trouble making videos, here are a couple of key advantages you can get from making videos this year:

- Drive traffic to your site

- Have your organization appear in Google list items

- Improve your consumer loyalty

- Improve customers' interaction with your website

- Create more intelligent clients and clients

- Grow your business

CHAPTER 2

Steps to making Great Training Video

The most effective method to making great and effective instructional or training videos

In this chapter and subsequent chapters, I'll take you through key strides to making effective training videos.

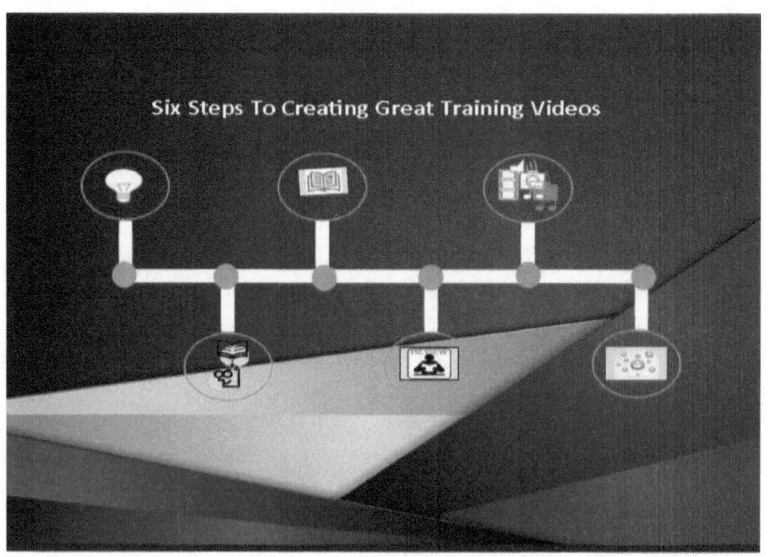

I'll talk about the sorts of video you can make, and how you can alter them in manners that catch and keep viewers still watching.

OK let's begin!

The first step is to pick your topic or area of focus

The principal activity when making training videos is to choose a helpful, pertinent point. These days, individuals rush to relinquish videos that don't give the pertinent data, so choosing a subject that is salient, intriguing and significance to your crowd is basic.

To choose the correct subject, first, characterize who your crowd will be.

At that point build up a careful comprehension of your crowd and their needs. Set aside some effort to investigate and recognizes the topic they're generally intrigued by or need assistance mostly in. Tailor your examination techniques to the area and size of your intended customer.

In the event that your task is to train your clients, at that point you may direct meetings with them.

In the case where you're making documentation for a bigger crowd, at this point a thorough study may be a perfect method to gather data.

Consider the accessibility of online discussions and different assets as an approach to direct you in refining your point.

How to make great training videos

Sharpen your subject to a solitary, centred thought. In case you're experiencing difficulty doing that, think about breaking it into two subjects, with the second structure on the first.

A series gives an amazing method to make instructional video that are valuable and simple to understand.

CHAPTER 3

Various Format that your training videos that can be.

The next stage in making an effective training video is to pick a format. As you begin to take a thought at the video, consider the assets accessible, your course of events, and customers' desires.

Various sorts of training videos take various degrees of time and effort to finish.

Here are a few formats you may decide to use for your training video.

How to make great training videos

Screencast

A screencast is a chronicle of your PC screen. In the event that you are preparing individuals on another product or PC software usage, this will probably be the best format of your video. Screencasts can extend from casual to profoundly-clean creations.

Moderator video

For live training, think about making a moderator video. After this, you can edit and use it as a feature of your training video.

In a case where you're training individuals on forms, an item demo video format might be the correct decision. In these recordings, somebody normally goes about as a "host" and shows the watchers how a specific item, administration, or procedure utilizes this format to a great deal.

Microvideo

A microvideo is a short video – five to fifteen seconds – that shows a simple procedure or thought on a topic. In some cases microvideos don't have narrations but rather depend on visuals or text on the screen. This may be a decent decision if what you want is to create various straightforward contents that don't occupy sufficient time or warrant making a more extended training video.

Role Play Video

In a role play video, a situation is carried on to assist watchers with imagining and better comprehend the manner in which a specific set of events ought to go. They are useful for traing workers or clients on the most proficient method to deal with things like deals calls, specialized help forms, and other social cooperation.

It takes a touch of acting. This format is consider may be the smartest option in the case of soft skill training as it assists customers with imagining genuine conditions and circumstances.

Animation Format

Here, animated video which uses text and designs to communicate as the need should arise. They take some specialized and imaginative expertise to make, however they're incredible for connecting with your clients or customers.

Intuitive video

Intuitive or interactive videos are a more up to date video format and design. One approach to think about these resembles a "state your own experience" video where viewers are encouraged to react to circumstances and afterward perceive how things play out contingent upon their choice. They can be a decent method to get your client included.

In the event that you need individuals to encounter how various choices play out, you may check out this.

How to make great training videos

CHAPTER 4

Scripting and Storyboarding

Make the Script and storyboard of your training video.

This is the next step in creating your training video

Once you start pondering your video, a reasonable picture rises in your mind. The scenes design is pictures all together, the visuals are perfect, and the words simply should be said out loud. It becomes

How to make great training videos

Obvious that we didn't plan, if you go directly to recording your video with no prep work, it turns out to be certain that these things are not as sorted out and immaculate as they show up in our creative mind.

I know this because I have done it. Because we can't go directly to creating a video, doesn't mean we don't really have an extraordinary video as a top priority.

It just exhibits the significance of getting those words, visuals, and scenes on the mind onto paper as a content with scenes as well as storyboard.

The first and most significant prep task is to compose a content. Start a report in your preferred word processor and begin composing what you need to state.

In case you're doing a screencast or microvideo that includes screen accounts, experience the procedure you intend to appear. It may assist with considering how you'd clarify the procedure on the off chance that somebody from your crowd was sitting with you.

In the wake of scripting, make a storyboard. A storyboard shows the visual grouping of a video through straightforward portrays or pictures.

I usually take couples of screen captures or take pictures to get a solid thought of what I need to appear in my video. Your storyboard shouldn't take long to assemble, and you don't have to struggle with drawing anything excellent. Stick figures work fine and dandy.

This progression will give you a superior thought of your general video length before you start recording or altering.

CHAPTER 5

Recording and Editing

Okay, when you've done all the prep work, you can begin recording. You don't need to be a video expert to get extraordinary video, either. Anybody can record a brilliant screencast with only a little practice. What's more, you likely have the innovation in your pocket (Hint: cell phone camera) to record an incredible video on the off chance that you've decided to do a pretend or demonstration video.

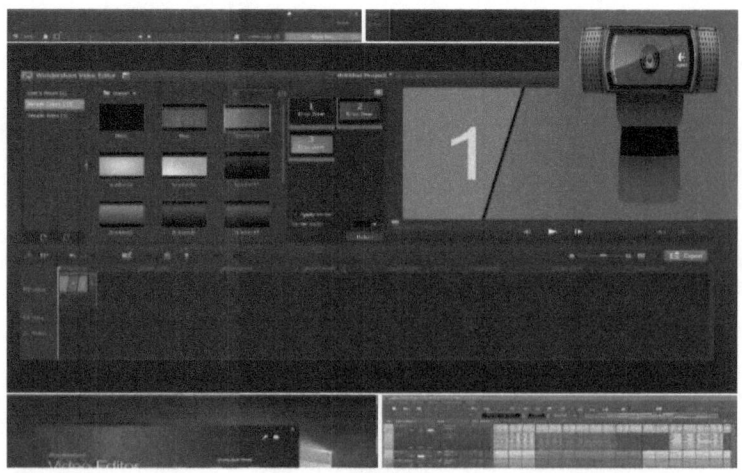

How to make great training videos

When you've recorded your recording, there are various approaches to edit your video so it's outwardly captivating.

You can take advantage of some existing templates and layouts

Utilize a video introduction, outro, and lower thirds layouts that can be edited to coordinate content and brand Standard.

TechSmith Assets is another method to use in editing your video

At this point you can pick from more than half a million assets, like animations, moving backgrounds, pictures, and music to give your media the best effect possible.

Use of Annotations

In screencasts and different recordings, annotations are an incredible method to cause viewers to notice specific things. Arrows and shape callouts can even be joined with animation and text to keep watchers' attention where it should be.

Text overlays

Setting text on your video helps you keep things outwardly captivating while at the same time pounding home key focuses. Use it in lower thirds designs to present speakers or underline a point or thought.

Animation

Make text and shapes move into your video or along the screen. Animations are astounding for keeping visuals differed and interesting in your learning videos.

Custom animations are one choice; however Camtasia Behaviors are simple methods to rapidly add or inventively give life to text, shapes, and different designs in your videos.

Show the speaker

Try not to be hesitant to show the storyteller in your recordings. In screencasts, this is finished by recording your webcam and afterward changing to that recording at perfect minutes, for the most part the start and end.

Simply be certain you're looking into the camera!

You can as well include some collaboration

Collaboration is a strategy that is picking up footing in corporate training videos. With intuitive hotspots, you can send viewers to a particular point in a video, request that they react to info or guide viewers on what to do in subsequent video.

CHAPTER 6

Review and emphasis

When you have an early draft video, perhaps the best activity is to have partners or associates who can help review your video content.

A video audit will tell you whether you're in good shape and take into consideration rectifications, if need be, before you close to a last piece. It's consistently simpler to make changes at these early stages.

Moreover, having different eyes investigate your piece is the most ideal approach to guarantee there are no mix-ups like grammatical mistakes or flaw in the final project.

At the point when you're prepared to get an audit, you can transfer your draft video to TechSmith Video Review, which makes it simple to set up a proficient and successful criticism

At that point, welcome individuals to audit it or empower the open connect to send to a review of individuals. Commentators can leave remarks, increase the video with shapes, bolts or text, and react to each other, all inside Video Review.

At the point when analysts have completed the process of giving criticism, utilize their remarks to repeat on your underlying video, confirming the recommendations as you address them in your venture. When the entirety of the criticism has been fused, revisit the input circle, transferring the new form of your video for another round of input.

Criticism and survey are two of the best approaches to make an extraordinary video, so make your time on this stride. It might bode well to experience it two or even multiple times to ensure your video is perfect.

CHAPTER 7

Creating, hosting, and Publishing your video.

At long last, we've made it to the last step of making a great and first class training video: creation and hosting. This is the prime time when we make the video accessible to our watchers or clients.

The main activity is to create the video. Delivering your video renders it from the video proof-reader into a video record. You've likely known about various video document positions, particularly the most well-known and generally utilized MP4. Except if you have an explanation not to, I recommend delivering your video as a MP4 at a similar size you edited it.

When the video is created, it's now an ideal time to host it.

Hosting is the manner by which a video is made accessible to viewers or clients. YouTube and Vimeo are instances of hosting platforms, yet there are various different approaches to host a video, and it's critical to pick the one that works best for you.

In the event that you need to make your video open, I would recommend making a YouTube video. YouTube is extraordinary for learning content. Be that as it may, on the off chance that you need it to be accessible just to individuals or workers at your organization you can have it on your organization's assistance work area, information base, or site.

Another alternative is to utilize Screencast.com, which permits you to have videos and pictures, and afterward share a link with others. On the off chance that you made your video with Camtasia, you can even create videos directly to Screencast.com, YouTube, or Vimeo.

By now I want to believe you're prepared to make your own training videos!

How to make great training videos

CHAPTER 8

Frequently Ask Question and Answer Section

What is a Training video?

An internet training video, regardless of whether for worker training or client training, is a video devoted to instructing them on a particular topic with the view of showing an expertise or giving information on how to solve certain issues or challenge.

How would you make powerful training video?

The main intention for make a great preparing video is to ensure the theme or topic of discussion is important and relatable to the audience. Likewise, things like special visualizations, music, and different reviews, help, make the video intriguing and educational.

Where would I be able to host a Training video?

Hosting is the means by which a video is made accessible to viewers. YouTube and Facebook, Vimeo, Instagram are platforms of hosting your videos, however there are various different approaches to hosting your video content depending on the platform. It's essential to pick the one that works best for you.

Would i be able to utilize YouTube for training Videos?

Yes, In the event that you need to make your video open, YouTube video is the best. YouTube is incredible for learning content. Facebook and Instagram group are also some open platforms for hosting you training video. But in the case where you need it to be accessible to just some individuals at your organization you can have it on your organization's assistance work area, information base, or site or evening messaging platform like WhatsApp Messenger, Facebook messenger, Imo, telegram and other instant messaging platforms

How would you make a training video?

You needn't have a ton of experience or be a video expert to effectively make a training video. You simply need a camera or screen recorder, a decent mouthpiece, and some video altering software installed on your device or PC.